❖❖❖ The WRIE

PAGE	CITY	STRUCTURE
9	LOS ANGELES	Aline Barnsdall House ✶ (Hollyhock House)
13	PASADENA	Alice Millard House (La Miniatura)
17	LOS ANGELES	Charles Ennis House ✶
21	HOLLYWOOD	Samuel Freeman House ✶
25	HOLLYWOOD	John Storer House
29	BEVERLY HILLS	Anderton Court Shops ✶
33	BRENTWOOD	George D. Sturges House
37	MALIBU	Arch Oboler Gatehouse/Studio
41	MONTECITO	George C. Stewart House
44	Area Maps	
47	SAN LUIS OBISPO	Kundert Medical Clinic ✶
51	CARMEL	Clinton Walker House
55	PALO ALTO	Paul and Jean Hanna House ✶ (Honeycomb House)
59	ATHERTON	Arthur C. Mathews House
63	SAN FRANCISCO	V. C. Morris Gift Shop ✶
67	SAN ANSELMO	Robert Berger House
71	SAN RAFAEL	Marin County Civic Center ✶
75	BERKELEY	Hilary and Joe Feldman House
79	REDDING	Pilgrim Congregational Church ✶
82	Other Sites	
83	Ancillary Buildings	

✶Indicates sites open to the public or where regularly scheduled or limited and special tours are offered, as noted in this guide book. The others are private residences that can be viewed from the road.

FINDING ALL THE WRIGHT PLACES IN CALIFORNIA

SECOND EDITION

Henry J. Michel

Finding All The WRIGHT Places In California
Second Edition, 1996

Copyright ©1996 Henry J. Michel
All Rights Reserved

Published by H. J. Michel Publishing Services
4842 Tilden Ave., Sherman Oaks, CA 91423
818- 789-1410

ISBN 0-9652237-0-1

Cover art and typography by Gary D. Schneider

Map art by Nonnette Sherry

Printed in USA

Page 3—Name plate at the doorway of
Frank Lloyd Wright's first studio
in Oak Park, Illinois

THIS GUIDE to buildings in California designed by Frank Lloyd Wright is suited for use by visitors from out of town or from out of the country as well as local residents living near some of the sites.

For visitors unfamiliar with the State's road system, the maps and instructions relate each site to the closest, most logical interstate and freeway routes. From these the way is shown street by street and turn by turn to each location.

Visitors living in and familiar with the Bay Area or Los Angeles, where several sites are clustered, can adjust their approaches depending on their starting points. They will find the detailed street-by-street instructions most useful for them.

The prescribed routes are designed to provide the easiest (and usually shortest) access to each site. Attention was given to usual traffic conditions and ease in finding key points along the way. The navigational problems facing the driver unfamiliar with the area were fully considered.

Whether you are a local or a tourist from afar, it is suggested that a good road map of California and the major metropolitan areas be used along with the guide.

Half of the sites are accessible by guided or self-guided tours. Tour days and hours vary and can change. Schedules in this guide were current at publication time. It is wise to verify by phone before traveling long distances to a site.

The other sites detailed in the guide are private residences. Their inclusion does not imply that visitors may intrude on the owner's privacy. The publisher does not recommend nor encourage trespassing on these properties. Each house can be viewed from the road.

EXPLANATION OF CODES, ABBREVIATIONS AND DATA

ROADS
I–xx   Interstate Highway
US xx   Numbered U.S. Highway
SR xx   Numbered State Route
(xx)   County road numbers

In order to show important details of the routings, maps may not necessarily depict distances to scale.

LEGEND
R   Right turn
L   Left turn
▲   Frank Lloyd Wright site

Fractional miles are shown in tenths (0.4, 1.3).

Each residence is identified by the name of Wright's client; the public buildings by their original names.

The dating of each building is based on several widely available sources which sometimes offer conflicting dates. Some sources may denote the completion date while others may refer to design date. Dates presented herein are those more likely to denote when the building was essentially completed.

Wright in California

Frank Lloyd Wright (1867-1959) left his native Wisconsin at the age of nineteen. Within two years he was on his way to becoming the head draftsman in the highly respected Chicago architectural firm of Adler and Sullivan—a most fortunate combination of partners for him to work under.

Louis H. Sullivan, exponent of the "form follows function" approach to spatial design, was his mentor. Dankmar Adler was outstanding in his engineering abilities. Wright had an unusual ability to absorb quickly and build upon all that he learned from these teachers.

It must have been that way, for he had only a smattering of formal training in any of the related disciplines. Like many others who became architects in those times, Wright endured several years of apprenticeship; a system he later employed at his Taliesin schools in Wisconsin and Arizona.

By the second decade of the century he had become well known, even controversial, in his profession. He had created a body of work sufficiently unique to have its own name; Prairie Houses, concentrated largely in Illinois, Wisconsin and Michigan. By the 1920s he was probing new ideas.

His early California work was transitional for his career. Hollyhock House (1920–21) which he may have first conceived as a poured concrete structure became instead a more conventional stucco-walled edifice with cast concrete bases and ornament. It was a pivotal work in the architect's career, as he broke away from the brick and wood residences of his Prairie style.

He experimented with concrete, even under the primitive building methods available for the Imperial Hotel work in Japan. He had his son, Lloyd, supervise the building of his four *textile block* houses in California.

With his work in Japan finished, he attempted to build a practice in California, looking to a new group of clients, many associated with the arts, and perhaps more open to new concepts. But a successful practice failed to develop there and Wright eventually re-established himself in Wisconsin with his winter quarters in Arizona.

Over his last thirty years he added to his body of work in California. Clustered mainly in the Los Angeles and San Francisco Bay areas, these buildings make up the largest concentration of his designs except for those in and around Chicago, southeast Wisconsin and in Arizona.

This book is a guide to those wonderful California sites.

On the next page a parade of Frank Lloyd Wright's buildings in California begins. Each has its own distinct character.

The sites extend from Pasadena, across the Los Angeles area, then sweeping northwest to the Bay Area. On the maps of the center pages one can envision a continuous line, city to city. The order of presentation varies only slightly from this.

Hollyhock House has been taken out of line and presented first. There are good reasons for setting this house apart.

It was the first of Wright's buildings completed in Southern California. Only one other preceded it in the state.
It marked a watershed in his career; a clear break from his earlier residential style, the renowned Prairie Houses. He was in an experimental period; in a new environment, using new materials and methods, and often dealing with a different type of client.

Of the more than four hundred Wright buildings completed, seventeen have been recommended by the American Institute of Architects and the National Trust for Historic Preservation to be forever preserved. Hollyhock House and two other California buildings are among those so selected.

Finally, it is the only Frank Lloyd Wright building in the state that currently operates as a house museum with regular daily docent-guided tours.

For these reasons Hollyhock House is placed at the head of the parade. Included throughout the pages of this guide are miniature photo-details of many of its features.

ALINE BARNSDALL HOUSE (1920-21)

"Hollyhock House" in Barnsdall Park

❖❖❖ Wright broke from his midwestern Prairie House mode and entered a period of experimentation. A key building in Wright's career, this stucco-walled house is trimmed with cast concrete ornamentation. Wright called it a "California Romanza." ❖❖❖

ALINE BARNSDALL HOUSE

"Hollyhock House" in Barnsdall Park
4808 Hollywood Blvd. — Los Angeles

LOCATION — Barnsdall Park is near the intersection of Hollywood Blvd. and Vermont Ave., just east of Hollywood. Park entrance is on Hollywood Blvd.

DIRECTIONS — **From US 101 (Hollywood Fwy.)** —
North: Exit Vermont Ave., turn **R**, go 1.5 mi. to Hollywood Blvd. turn **L**. Park entrance is at left about 1 block west.
South: Exit Hollywood Blvd., turn **L**, go 1.5 mi. to park entrance just past Edgemont Ave. Turn **R** into park.
From I-5 (Golden State Fwy.) —
North or South: Exit Los Feliz Blvd. turn west, go 2.25 mi. to Vermont Ave., south 0.5 mi. to Hollywood Blvd., turn **R**. Park entrance is on the left about 1 block west.

PARKING — There are free parking areas along the one-way road circling the hilltop park.

ACCESSIBILITY — Open to the public on guided tours daily (except Mon.) at noon, 1, 2, and 3 p.m. Entrance fees are nominal. Large or non-English speaking groups should call in advance (213) 485-4581 for arrangements.

The adjacent guest house, modified by architect R. M. Schindler from Wright's plans, now serves as the Barnsdall Art Center and is not open to tours.

PHOTOGRAPHY — The tour affords opportunity for interior and exterior photography.

ALINE BARNSDALL HOUSE

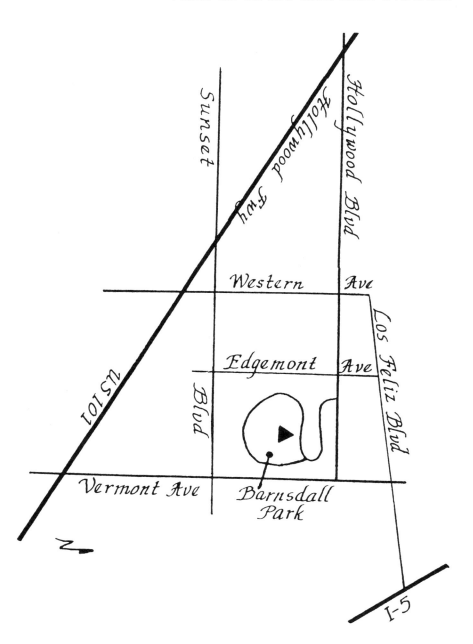

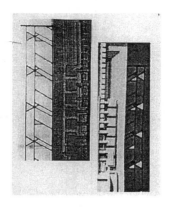

Glass panels and concrete pillars
Hollyhock House

ALICE MILLARD HOUSE (1923)

"La Miniatura"

❖❖❖ The first of Wright's concrete block experiments. The Millards were earlier Wright clients in Illinois. The widow needed a small home and library for their valuable book collection. The plain, patterned or perforated (to allow light) blocks evidence Wright's awareness of Mayan designs. The studio addition at the rear is by his son, Lloyd. ❖❖❖

ALICE MILLARD HOUSE

"La Miniatura"
645 Prospect Crescent — Pasadena

LOCATION — Pasadena is about ten miles northeast of downtown Los Angeles.

DIRECTIONS — **From I-210 (Foothill Fwy) West** — Pick up 134 Fwy. briefly then exit at Orange Gove Blvd. and turn **R** onto Orange Grove. Go north 0.7 mi. to Rosemont Ave. Continue north 1 blk. and turn **L** at the stone-pillared entrance of Prospect Blvd. Drive about 0.5 mi. to Prospect Crescent, turn **L** and the house is in view.
From SR-134 (Ventura Fwy) East — Exit at Orange Grove Blvd. and turn **L** and proceed 0.7 mi. on Orange Grove to Rosemont Ave. Continue north 1 blk.: turn **L** at stone-pillared entrance of Prospect Blvd. Drive about 0.5 mi. to Prospect Crescent, turn **L** and the house is in view.

ACCESSIBILITY — This is a private residence. View the front from Prospect Crs. Seen from Rosemont is the studio and pond.

PARKING — O.K. on Prospect Crs. but not on Rosemont. Use Prospect Terrace, just to the north, and walk a block down Rosemont.

PHOTOGRAPHY — Good views of facade and entrance areas, but difficult to shoot the back from the Rosemont side. Telephoto lens can help.

ALICE MILLARD HOUSE

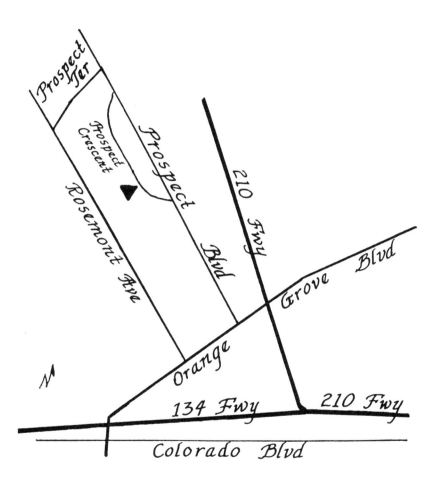

Art glass windows
Hollyhock House

CHARLES ENNIS HOUSE (1924)

❖❖❖ The last of Frank Lloyd Wright's "textile block" houses proves to be surprisingly small, given its massive, fortress-like visage upon approach. This startlingly different home with a spectacular view has been used in several movie and television productions. ❖❖❖

CHARLES ENNIS HOUSE
2607 Glendower Ave. — Los Angeles

LOCATION — The house is just south of the Griffith Observatory and Greek Theater sections of Griffith Park, between the I-5 and US 101 freeways. It is within view of Hollyhock House a mile to the south.

DIRECTIONS — (See Hollyhock House map on page 11 for approaches to the area.) From the Vermont Ave.-Los Feliz Blvd. juction proceed north of Los Feliz on the divided roadway. At 0.1 mi. Gainsborough Rd. comes in from the right. Go another hundred yards, turn L where Cromwell St. crosses the center parkway and southbound lanes and meets Glendower Rd. Turn R up Glendower 0.6 mi. to the address.

PARKING — Parking on the narrow street is severely restricted.

ACCESSIBILITY — All tours are by reservation only. This private residence offers public tours on the second Saturday in January, March, May, July. September and November. The fee includes transportation to the house from a nearby parking area—$10 adults, $5 seniors, students, youngsters (child in arms free). Call 213-668-0234 for information and reservation.

Special tours for schools, architectural groups and out of town visitors—$10 per person with a three person (or $30) minimum.

PHOTOGRAPHY — Several aspects of the exterior can be shot from spots along the road. Tours allow exterior photography only. Special photography tours by appointment.

CHARLES ENNIS HOUSE

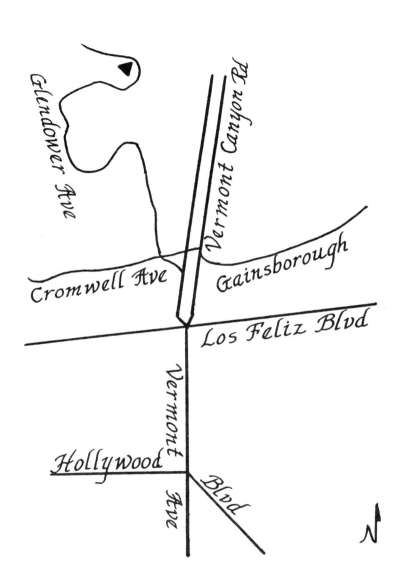

Cast concrete rooftop finial
Hollyhock House

SAMUEL FREEMAN HOUSE (1924)

❖❖❖ The smallest of Wright's "textile block" houses. Abundant use of perforated blocks and the unusual corner window designs provide openness and light in this house which is perched on the edge of a steep hill overlooking Los Angeles.

    The house is now owned by the University of Southern California and is being restored by the School of Architecture. ❖❖❖

SAMUEL FREEMAN HOUSE

1962 Glencoe Way. — Hollywood

LOCATION — In Hollywood near the intersection of Highland Ave. and Hollywood Blvd., about a quarter mile south of the Hollywood Bowl, off US 101.

DIRECTIONS — **From US 101 (Hollywood Fwy) —
South:** Exit onto Highland Ave, proceed 0.5 mi., get into far right lane which must turn **R** onto Franklin Ave. First street after turn is Hillcrest Ave. A right turn leads to Glencoe Way, two blocks up a steep hill. (See PARKING information below.)
North: Exit at Caheunga Blvd., turn **L** go one block to Franklin Ave. then **R**. Proceed west until Franklin meets Highland and jogs ½ block south. Move into far right lane to return to Franklin turning **R**. First street after turn is Hillcrest Ave. A right turn leads to Glencoe Way, two blocks up a steep hill. (See PARKING information.)

PARKING — On the steep streets north of Franklin parking is very limited. Consider using the streets below Franklin with time limit or meter parking. If walking is a problem, drive up, turn around where Glencoe makes a sharp left in front of the Freeman House, **(Driving beyond this point is not recommended)**. Park facing downhill on Glencoe or Hillcrest.

ACCESSIBILITY — Guided tours are conducted at 2 and 4 p.m. most Saturdays; call (213) 851-0671 for information. For groups of ten or more, reserve in advance. Fee is $10 (students $5). Tour visitors may use the lot of the Methodist Church on Franklin, just east of Hillcrest Rd.

PHOTOGRAPHY — Other than on tours, it is limited to the exterior near the entrance.

SAMUEL FREEMAN HOUSE

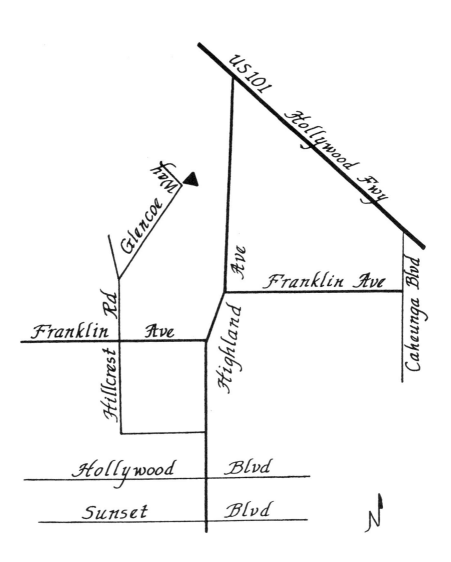

Chair
Hollyhock House

JOHN STORER HOUSE (1923-24)

❖❖❖ Second of Wright's four "textile block" houses. The massive block facade is accented by the wood-framed windows of a two-storied living room, giving it an imposing look. The recently added security wall along the street matches the blocks of the house. ❖❖❖

JOHN STORER HOUSE

8161 Hollywood Blvd. — Hollywood

LOCATION — At the west end of Hollywood where Hollywood Blvd. is a curvy, residential street in the hills west of Laurel Canyon Blvd.

DIRECTIONS — **From US 101 North** — Exit Sunset Blvd. and proceed west 3.0 mi. *or* **US 101 South** — Exit Vine St., **R** 3 blk. to Sunset, turn **R**, go west 2.2 mi.
Then:
At Cresecent Heights Blvd. go one block beyond to Selma Ave. and turn **R**. Drive 0.2 mi. to Crescent Hts. where a sharp left sends you up around two curves to Hollywood Blvd. (It may be unsigned). Turn **R**, go about 100 yds. and **R** again. The house is directly in front of you. (Note: Approach via Hollywood Blvd. from the east is not recommended.)
Coming from the north, you can use Laurel Canyon Blvd. As you exit the hills, shunt to the right onto Hollywood Blvd., up the ramp-like street, around a curve or two and the house is right there.

PARKING — On the street.

ACCESSIBILITY — This is a private residence.

PHOTOGRAPHY — Offers a virtually unobstructed view of the facade from the street.

JOHN STORER HOUSE

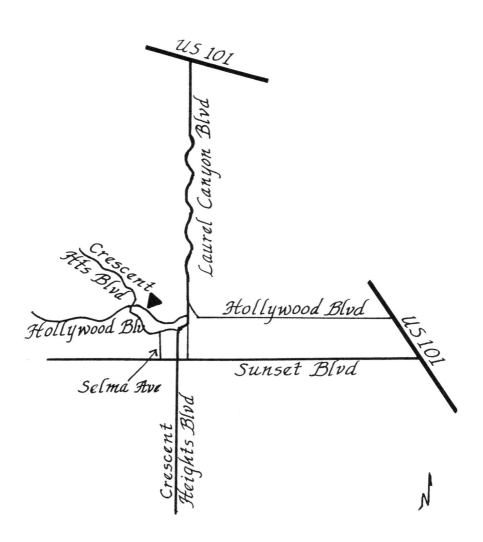

Art glass enclosure, play porch
Hollyhock House

ANDERTON COURT SHOPS (1952)

❖❖❖ Wright often used ramps to move people in public buildings. He connects floor levels by their use here. The serrated pylon resembles the one on his Marin County Civic Center. His use of the circle, which can be seen in some of the shop windows, is characteristic only of the later part of his career. ❖❖❖

ANDERTON COURT SHOPS

332 Rodeo Drive — Beverly Hills

LOCATION — Beverly Hills is about eight miles west of the Los Angeles Civic Center.

DIRECTIONS— The map locates the 300 block of Rodeo Dr. between Dayton and Brighton. Be alert to No Turn signs and One Way traffic. Here are approaches to the area:
From the I-405 (San Diego Fwy) - (1) Exit at Sunset Blvd., drive east to Beverly Dr., turn R, continue past Santa Monica Blvd. to streets shown on map. or — (2) Exit at Wilshire Blvd., drive east to the 9600 block as shown.
From the I-10 (Santa Monica Fwy) - Exit at La Cienega Blvd., drive north to Wilshire, turn L (west) and go to the 9600 block and the streets shown on map.

PARKING — During business hours parking may be difficult. With luck you can park behind the Court Shops. There is metered parking on most streets, free off-street city-owned lots in the area and private lots too.

ACCESSIBILITY — You can wander through the Court's passageways even before or after shopping hours.

PHOTOGRAPHY — To get just the architecture without the obstructing traffic, early morning (especially Sunday) is a good time. But natural light is best on the facade in late afternoon.

ANDERTON COURT SHOPS

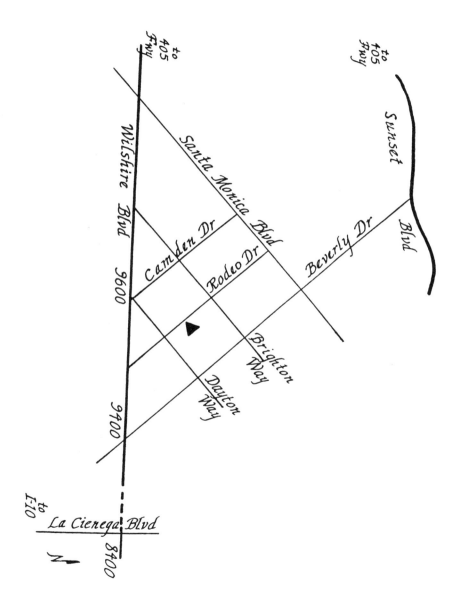

Art stone pillars, living room wall screen
Hollyhock House

GEORGE D. STURGIS HOUSE (1939)

❖❖❖ The cube-like structure, suspended out from the hillside slope, is a stunning sight. The brick base growing out of the hill supports the superstructure with its cantilevered terrace enclosed by rough redwood walls. ❖❖❖

GEORGE D. STURGIS HOUSE

449 Skyewiay Road. — Brentwood

LOCATION — Brentwood is located in the northwest corner of the Los Angeles basin, just west of the 405 Fwy. and about two miles north of the I-10

DIRECTIONS — From I-405 (San Diego Fwy) - Exit at Sunset Blvd. and go west on Sunset 1 mi. Turn **R** onto Kenter Ave. and drive 0.7 mi. to where Bonhill Rd. and Skyewiay Rd. meet Kenter. Best approach is up Bonhill to where it meets Skyewiay again. A sharp **R** turn puts you on the side of Skyewiay where parking is allowed. The house is just a few yards past the turn.

PARKING — Street parking is OK on the west (downhill traffic) side of Skyewiay but not the other side in this block.

ACCESSIBILITY — This is a private residence. Much of the exterior, however, can be viewed from the road.

PHOTOGRAPHY — This spectacular structure, projecting from its hillside site can be shot from many angles along the inclined street.

GEORGE D. STURGIS HOUSE

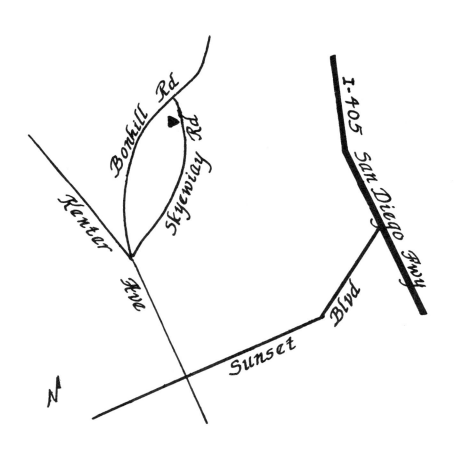

Torchere, living room
Hollyhock House

ARCH OBOLER GATEHOUSE and STUDIO (1941)

❖❖❖ The famous radio and screen writer of the '30s and '40s did not finish his planned estate. The main house, *Eaglefeather*, to be perched on the ridge of a mountain with a view of the Pacific ocean was not built.

Only the studio-retreat (above) and the gatehouse (p. 84) were completed. Built of rubblestone-embedded concrete and redwood walls, the two buildings are superb examples of Wright's skill in mating structure with site. This long-neglected property is now undergoing restorative measures by its new owner. ❖❖❖

ARCH OBOLER GATEHOUSE and STUDIO

32436 Mulholland Hwy. — Malibu

LOCATION — In the mountains high above the famed Malibu coastal colony, the Oboler site is more easily approached by the inland route via US 101. It is some 37 miles northwest of the Los Angeles Civic Center, about 6 miles south of Westlake Village.

DIRECTIONS — **From US 101 North or South** — Exit onto Westlake Blvd. (SR 23), proceed south through Westlake Village for five miles to juncture with Mulholland Hwy. Turn L (east) onto Mulholland and drive 1.5 mi. to address on the mail box where the gatehouse can be seen across a narrow ravine. From a spot about 500 yards up the road one sees the studio high on a peak.
As An Alternate Route — If starting from coastal areas west of Los Angeles, you may wish to use Pacific Coast Hwy. and either Mulholland or SR 23 (Decker Rd.).

PARKING — Roadside parking where the shoulder allows. The traffic is light, but fast vehicles dictate caution.

ACCESSIBILITY — This private property can be viewed from the road.

PHOTOGRAPHY — For the studio a telephoto lens is needed. Early morning is best, as later shadows and back lighting obliterate details.

ARCH OBOLER GATEHOUSE and STUDIO

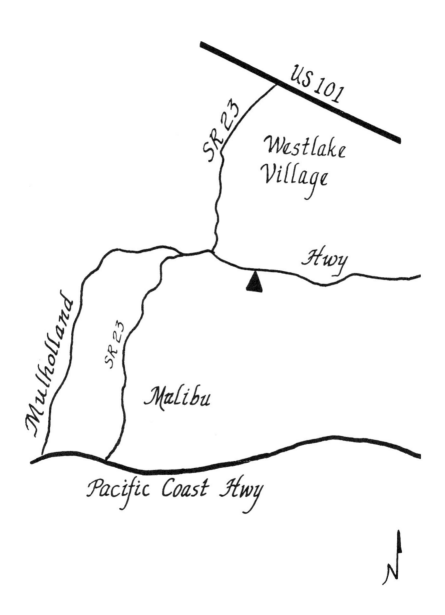

Concrete planter
Hollyhock House

GEORGE C. STEWART HOUSE (1909)

❖❖❖ This first Wright-designed home built in California was for an earlier Midwest client, and it echoes Wright's Prairie style. He was not involved in its construction and it has been much modified over the years. Its redwood exterior lends a Craftsman-like touch to what in brick and stone would have suited it for a site facing Lake Michigan rather than the Pacific, a view now obscured by giant trees. ❖❖❖

GEORGE C. STEWART HOUSE

196 Hot Springs Road — Montecito

LOCATION — Montecito is located just south of Santa Barbara on US 101.

DIRECTIONS — **From US 101 North** - Use the Olive Mill Rd./Coastal Village Rd. exit ramp, Go straight ahead onto Coastal Village Rd., 0.7 mi. to Hot Springs Rd. and turn **R** then a short distance (past Palm Tree Ln. and Hermosilla Dr.) up to Summit Rd. Turn **R** on Summit; the house is at your right. **From US 101 South** — Use Hot Springs Rd./Coastal Village Rd. exit. At end of ramp turn **L** onto Hot Springs Rd. a short distance (past Palm Tree Ln. and Hermosilla Dr.) up to Summit Rd. Turn **R** on Summit; the house is at your right.

PARKING — Park on Summit Rd. There's no parking on Hot Springs Rd.

ACCESSIBILITY — This is a private residence. Viewing is from the street.

PHOTOGRAPHY — There is an unobstructed view of the front of the house from Summit Rd.

GEORGE C. STEWART HOUSE

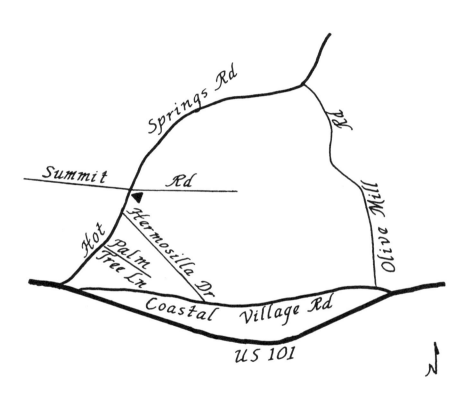

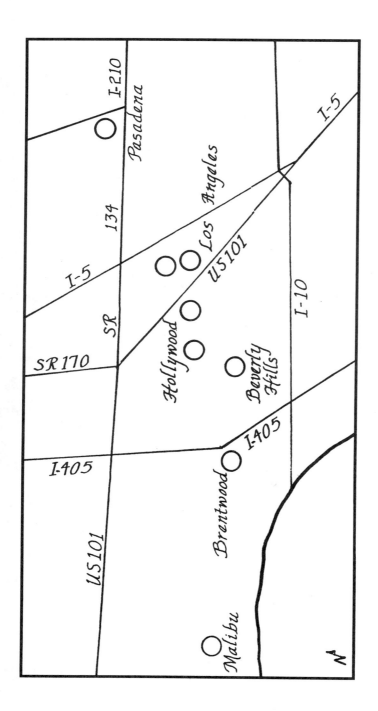

Los Angeles Area Locations

California Locations

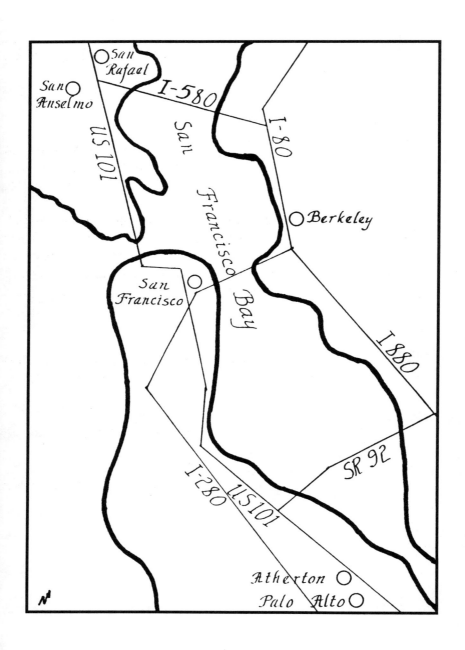

San Francisco Bay Area Locations

KUNDERT MEDICAL CLINIC (1954-56)

❖❖❖ Wright's client, Dr. Karl Kundert, still owns the building which has been recently restored and is occupied by another doctor. There's a mix of traditional Wright here – extensive use of brick, flat roof, patterned clerestory windows, a fireplace set in a ceiling-high brick wall. ❖❖❖

KUNDERT MEDICAL CLINIC

1106 Pacific Street — San Luis Obispo

LOCATION — San Luis Obispo is in the central coastal area midway between Santa Barbara and Monterey on US 101.

DIRECTIONS — **From US 101 North** — Exit at Marsh St., continue on Marsh 0.8 mi. to Santa Rosa Ave.; turn R. Go 1 block to Pacific St. and the building is at the left as you cross the bridge.
From US 101 South — Exit at Monterey St. and continue 0.8 mi. to Santa Rosa Ave. Turn L and go three blocks to Pacific St. It is on the corner to your left.

PARKING — Park on the street or in the clinic's lot at the far end of the building.

ACCESSIBILITY — Both doctors are empathetic with Wright aficionados. When the clinic is open, visitors are welcome to enter and view the reception/waiting area and to sign the visitor log.

PHOTOGRAPHY — All sides of the exterior as well as the waiting room are at your camera's disposal (but waiting patients are entitled to their privacy, please).

KUNDERT MEDICAL CLINIC

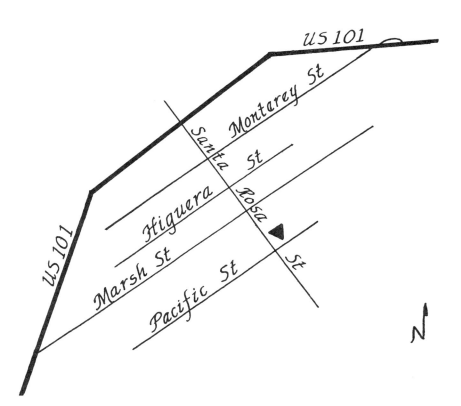

Art glass windows, owner's room
Hollyhock House

CLINTON WALKER HOUSE (1948)

❖❖❖ This stone and glass house with its angular ship-like shapes, set on coastal rocks jutting to the sea, combine for a spectacular sight. The patina-toned, layered metal roof brings to mind the wind-bent cypresses of the Monterey area. ❖❖❖

CLINTON WALKER HOUSE

Scenic Road at Santa Lucia Ave. — Carmel

LOCATION — Carmel is on the coast, just south of Monterey, midway between San Francisco and San Luis Obispo, west of Salinas.

DIRECTIONS — **From US 101 North** — At Salinas take SR 68 West 20 mi. to SR 1. Follow SR 1 about 5 mi. south to Carmel.
From US 101 South — Exit to SR 156 West (at Prunedale). Drive about 7 mi. on 156 which merges with SR 1 beyond Castroville; continue on SR 1 about 17 mi. to Carmel.
From SR 1 — You can enter the north end of Carmel at Carpenter St. or Ocean Ave., then go across town toward Scenic Rd. along the ocean. The house is beyond the end of the beach and park areas just below Santa Lucia Ave.
OR: continue south on SR 1 to Rio Rd. near the Mission. Turn R, go about 0.7 mi. to Santa Lucia Ave. then L to Scenic Rd. and L again.

PARKING — Allowed on Scenic Rd.

ACCESSIBILITY — This is a private residence.

PHOTOGRAPHY — The house can be shot from either side at road level or, when the tide is out, from various beach-level locations on either side of the promontory. There are stairs to the beach at the north side.

CLINTON WALKER HOUSE

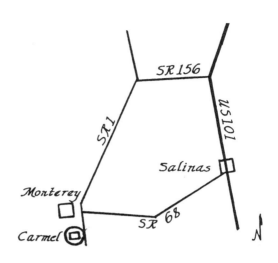

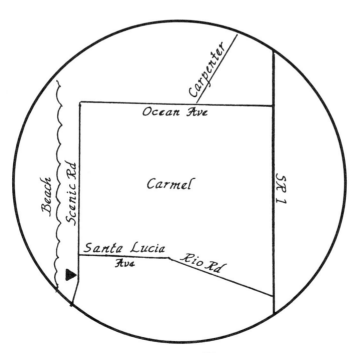

Lounge chair and hassock
Hollyhock House

PAUL and JEAN HANNA HOUSE (1936)

"Honeycomb House" at Stanford University

❖❖❖ Brick terrace walls form a base against the hillside for the lighter openness of the house's glass-panelled walls under nearly flat roofs. Its name derives from the hexagonal module used in its plan.

In a memorial at its 1960 national convention, the American Institute of Architects recommended that this and sixteen others of Wright's buildings be permanently preserved. ❖❖❖

PAUL and JEAN HANNA HOUSE

"Honeycomb House" at Stanford University
737 Frenchman's Road — Palo Alto

LOCATION — Palo Alto is some 30 miles south of San Francisco via US 101 or I-280. The house is on the Stanford campus and is owned by the University.

DIRECTIONS — **From US 101 (Bayshore Fwy) — North or South:** Exit Oregon Expressway (G3), proceed west on Oregon which at 1 mi. becomes Page Mill Rd. Continue another mile to Junipero Serra Blvd., turn **R** and proceed 1.5 mi. to East Campus Dr. **After entering campus at East Campus Dr. go 0.5 mi. to Mayfield Ave. and 0.4 mi. to Frenchman's Rd. A block or so on Frenchmen's to a 'Y' in the road and it's on the hill at your left.**

From I-280 (Junipero Serra Fwy) North — Exit at Page Mill Rd. (G3), go north 1 mi. to Junipero Serra Blvd., turn **L**, go 1.5 mi. to East Campus Dr. Then follow directions in bold type above.

From I-280 (Junipero Serra Fwy) South — Exit Sand Hill Rd., go east to Junipero Serra Blvd., turn **R**, go 0.7 mi. to East Campus Dr. Then follow directions in bold type above.

PARKING — Ample parking on Frenchman's Rd.

ACCESSIBILITY — Tours were indefinitely suspended after the '89 earthquake. Call (415) 723-3469 for information. A good view of the facade can be seen from the road. Binoculars help.

PHOTOGRAPHY — The front of the house can be shot from many positions on the street below and details can be picked up with a telephoto lens.

PAUL and JEAN HANNA HOUSE

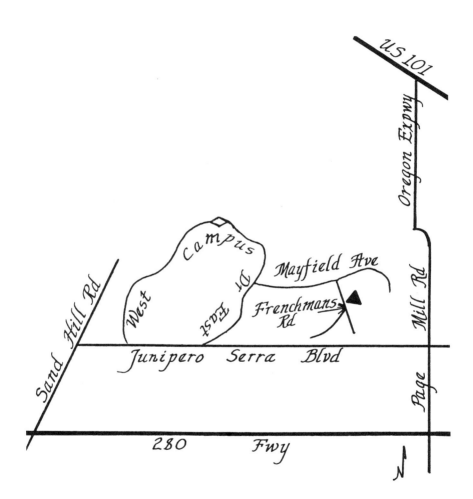

Cast concrete frieze
Hollyhock House

ARTHUR C. MATHEWS HOUSE (1950)

❖❖❖ The sand-toned brick wall under the low hip roof and broad eaves and a massive chimney can be seen from the road. A line of unconnected small windows, high on the wall, may seem an unusual facade, but on the garden side Wright utilized his more typical floor to ceiling glass in abundance. ❖❖❖

ARTHUR C. MATHEWS HOUSE

83 Wisteria Way — Atherton

LOCATION — Like nearby Palo Alto, Atherton is about 30 miles south of San Francisco on US 101. It is only about a half hour's drive from the Hanna house at Stanford University.

DIRECTIONS — **From US 101 (Bayshore Fwy)**- Either exit below can be used from north or south, so if the first one is missed catch the second one about two miles down the road. **North**: Exit Willow Rd. go west 1 mi. to Middlefield Rd. Turn **R**, proceed to Oak Grove and turn **R**. Go north to where Oak Grove meets Greenoaks Rd. Turn **L** here then **R** onto Rosewood Dr. and **R** again at the first street, Wisteria Way. **South**: Exit Marsh Rd., go west 1 mi. to Middlefield Rd., **L** 0.2 mi. to James Ave. **L** to Greenwood Dr., **R** 0.5 mi. to Rosewood Dr., turn **L**. Then the first **R** is Wisteria.

PARKING — No problem.

ACCESSIBILITY — This is a private residence.

PHOTOGRAPHY — Two sides of the house are in view from the street, but somewhat distant.

ARTHUR C. MATHEWS HOUSE

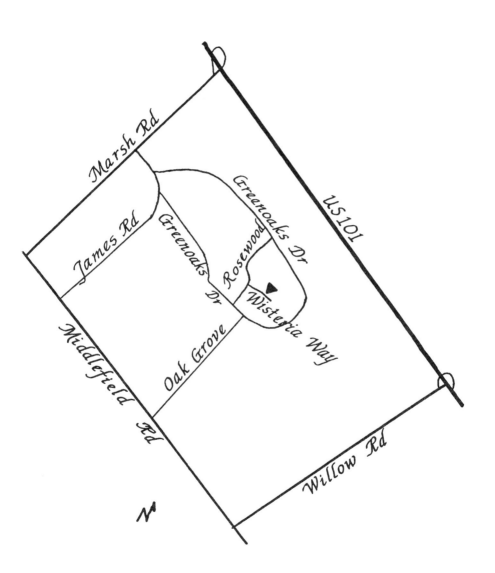

Wall light fixture
Hollyhock House

V. C. MORRIS GIFT SHOP (1948)

❖❖❖ Wright converted an existing building into this unique space for a retail shop (now an art gallery). His use of the arched entryway – seen in some of his early designs – was never more arresting than here where it balances and anchors the tall brick facade rising high above it.

It is one of three California buildings cited by the American Institute of Architects as representative of Wright's contribution to American culture. ❖❖❖

V. C. MORRIS GIFT SHOP

140 Maiden Lane — San Francisco

LOCATION — In the heart of San Francisco, just north of Market St. next to Union Square.

DIRECTIONS — **From US 101 North** — Transition to I-80 East, take Fourth St. exit onto Bryant, go 1 blk. to Third St., turn **L**. Go 4 blks. to junction of Market and Geary. Maiden Lane is half a block north of there.
From US 101 South — (Off the Golden Gate Bridge 101 is on surface streets.) From Van Ness Ave. (101) turn **L** on Post St. for 0.8 mi. to Stockton St. at Union Square. Maiden Lane is half a block south of there.
From I-80 West — From the East Bay area and beyond, use the San Francisco-Oakland Bay Bridge (I-80) to San Francisco. Exit Fifth St., **R** a block to Folsom St., **R** to Third St. and turn **L**. Go 4 blks. to junction of Market and Geary. Maiden Lane is half a block north of there.

PARKING — There's metered parking on many nearby streets, if you are lucky to find a spot. There are numerous fee parking garages in the area, both city-owned and private.

ACCESSIBILITY — Maiden Lane's two blocks have been made into a gated pedestrian mall. You may visit the gallery Monday – Saturday 10 AM – 6 PM, Sunday noon to 5 PM. Groups of ten or more by appointment only, 415-989-2100.

PHOTOGRAPHY — You may shoot the exterior, but photography is not allowed inside.

V. C. MORRIS GIFT SHOP

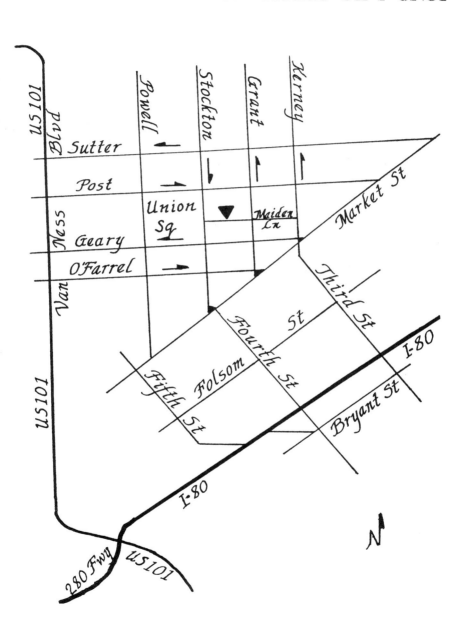

Living room skylight
Hollyhock House

ROBERT BERGER HOUSE (1950)

❖❖❖ This house derived from one of Wright's Usonian designs (a name he coined for an efficient, minimal house of moderate cost in which the owner could participate in the construction). This client took Wright's intentions to heart and built it himself of wood, glass, and concrete walls studded with native stone. ❖❖❖

ROBERT BERGER HOUSE

259 Redwood Road — San Anselmo

LOCATION — San Anselmo abuts San Rafael's old central city area, about 10 miles north of San Francisco. The house is not easy to find.

DIRECTIONS — **From US 101 North or South** – Use Central San Rafael exit. Take any of these streets going *west* that exit traffic and/or ramps allow you to use:
- 3rd. St. (1-way) runs into 2nd, then 4th.
- Mission St. to "H" St.; left 2 blks. to 4th.
- 4th St. will lead you into Red Mill Ave.

Continue on Red Mill past Drake Blvd. about 0.2 mi., turn **L** onto Madrone Ave. to Center then **R** another 0.3 mi. to Saunders St. Turn **L**, cross San Anselmo Ave. (just 50 ft.). Redwood Rd. is the norrow lane dead ahead. Go up the winding road to the address.

PARKING — No restrictions, but road is narrow, so a spot not blocking traffic is needed.

ACCESSIBILITY — This is a private residence. A limited view from the road exposes roof line and a portion of the facade. A less revealing view through the trees is from a spot about 50 yards down the road.

PHOTOGRAPHY — Limited from the road.

ROBERT BERGER HOUSE

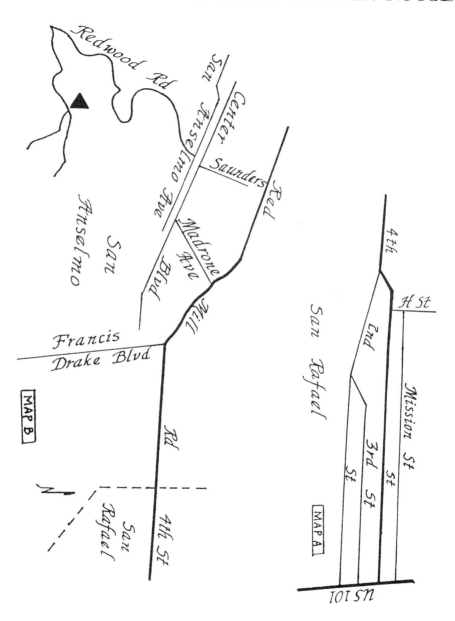

Fireplace art stone bas-relief
Hollyhock House

MARIN COUNTY CIVIC CENTER (1957–72)

❖❖❖ Containing the county's offices, its central library, the courts and even a jail, the huge two-winged building is set among rolling hills. Designed and begun before Wright's death, the complex was completed by others closely associated with him. The Administration Building was finished in 1962; the Hall of Justice in 1969. It is designated a National Historic Landmark.

Across Civic Center Drive is the Civic Center Post Office, Wright's only completed design for the U.S. Government. A quarter mile up the Drive is the Veterans' Memorial Auditorium (1972) which repeats the distinctive roof design of the Civic Center buildings (see Pg. 84). ❖❖❖

MARIN COUNTY CIVIC CENTER

3501 Civic Center Drive — San Rafael

LOCATION — San Rafael is 10 mi. north of San Francisco and the Golden Gate Bridge, on US 101.

DIRECTIONS — From US 101 North or South —
Take the N. San Pedro Rd. exit and head east. Turn L at first traffic signal east of the freeway; Civic Center Drive. The Center is there at your left.

PARKING — There are ample free parking areas surrounding the building.

ACCESSIBILITY — The Civic Center is open to the public during business hours, 9 AM to 4 PM, Monday – Friday. A free one-hour guided tour starts from the gift shop; second floor, Hall of Justice wing, 10:30 AM Tuesday – Friday. For special group tours by appointment call 415-472-7470.

The small post office building across Civic Center Dr. can be visited during business and open-lobby hours. The Veterans Memorial Auditorium is open only for scheduled performances and events.

PHOTOGRAPHY — This is a subject that will make an amateur photographer's day.

MARIN COUNTY CIVIC CENTER

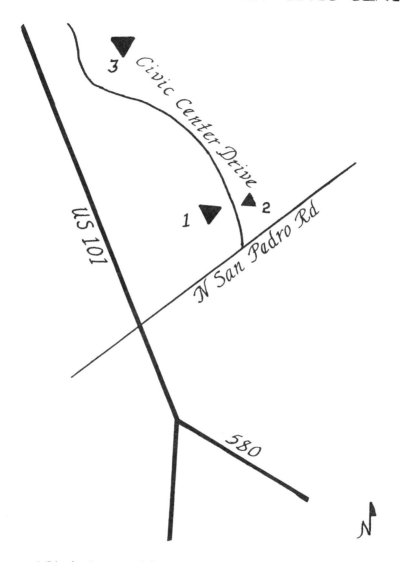

1 Marin County Civic Center
2 San Rafael Post Office
3 Veterans Memorial Auditorium

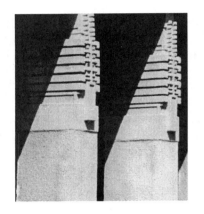

Colonnade
Hollyhock House

HILARY and JOE FELDMAN HOUSE (1974)

❖❖❖ Derived from one of Wright's unrealized Usonian plans for a Southern California site in the 1930's, this house is perched on a steep slope of the coastal hills offering a grand view of the bay. ❖❖❖

HILARY and JOE FELDMAN HOUSE

13 Mosswood Road. — Berkeley

LOCATION — Berkeley is just north of Oakland on the east side of San Francisco Bay.

DIRECTIONS — The key approach route is Interstate 80, reachable from all directions via the various connector links around the Bay area (280, 580, 880, etc.) depending on your line of approach.
From I-80 along the East Bay coast — Exit University Ave. and go east 2 mi. to Shattuck Ave. Go R 0.5 mi. to Channing Way, turn L. Drive 1 mi. to Channing's end at Prospect St and L on Prospect for one block.
Some 50 ft. south from the start of Panaramic Way you'll find Orchard Ln. consisting of several steep flights of stairs leading up to Mosswood Rd. A footpath also connects Mosswood to the stairway.

PARKING — Consider parking in the area of Channing and Prospect because continuing up Panaramic Way to Mosswood is difficult, norrow, and eventually dead-ended. In any case, it is necessary to walk the footpath for views of the house.

ACCESSIBILITY — This is a private residence.

PHOTOGRAPHY — The Mosswood side is heavily shaded, especially after the morning sun leaves. The views seen from the footpath have more light from midday on. Shots of the house are limited, but those from the footpath in the afternoon can be interesting.

HILARY and JOE FELDMAN HOUSE

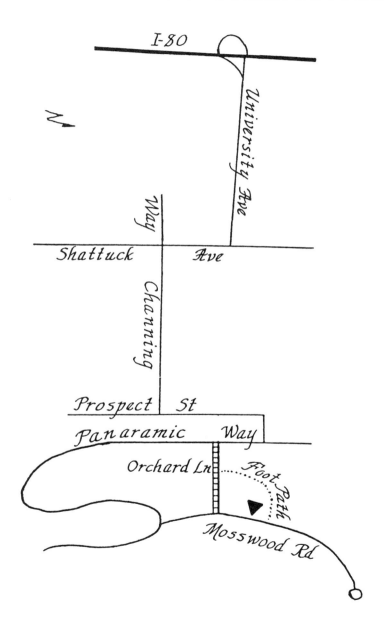

Dining room furniture
Hollyhock House

PILGRIM CONGREGATIONAL CHURCH
(1958–63)

❖❖❖ The full design, one of Wright's last, was never realized. The completed structure is under a white metal roof lined with a natural wood ceiling. The exterior and interior walls are of rough stone. But the most distinctive features are the angled concrete poles that bring to mind flying buttresses. ❖❖❖

PILGRIM CONGREGATIONAL CHURCH

2850 Foothill Blvd. — Redding

LOCATION — Redding is on I-5 some 170 mi. north of Sacramento.

DIRECTIONS — **From I-5** – At the juncture of SR 299 and SR 44 turn west on SR 299 toward central Redding. Here it feeds into westbound Shasta St. West on Shasta 1.1 mi. to Almond Ave. Turn **R**, go 2 blocks to Foothill Blvd. then **L** to the address.

PARKING — The church lot can be used.

ACCESSIBILITY — If the church building is locked, the office is usually staffed during business hours. Someone there will be glad to show you around or allow you to visit the interior where you can see Wright's drawings.

PHOTOGRAPHY — No restrictions.

PILGRIM CONGREGATIONAL CHURCH

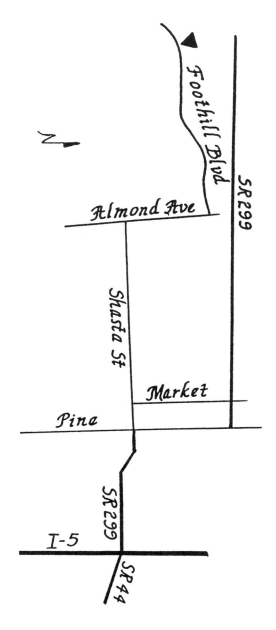

The California Wright houses listed below are not viewable from the public road. For that reason only they are not treated in detail in this guide. The omission is not meant to imply they are not worthy of visits by lovers of art and architecture. They are screened from casual view. The privacy of the owners of these homes as well as the other privately owned homes in this guide should be respected. Owners of Wright houses generally accommodate the needs of serious architectural scholars and professionals when requests for visits are made directly to them in advance.

Wilbur C. Pearce House
    5 Bradbury Hills Rd. Bradbury

Sidney Bazett House
    101 Reservoir Rd. Hillsborough

Maynard P. Buehler House
    6 Great Oak Cir. Orinda

Dr. and Mrs. George Ablin House
    4260 Country Club Dr. Bakersfield

Randall Fawcett House
    21200 Center Ave. Los Banos

Robert G. Walton House
    417 Hogue Road Modesto

ANCILLARY BUILDINGS—Some sites described in this book contain secondary structures that are either directly or indirectly related to Frank Lloyd Wright or to the principal building of the site. Four are shown on this and the following page.

BARNSDALL SITE, p. 10—"Residence A" guest house, 1921. Wright's design, with some modifications by R. M. Schindler. Now the Barnsdall Art Center.

MILLARD SITE, p. 13—Studio-library addition by Lloyd Wright completed in 1926.

OBOLER SITE, p. 37—The gatehouse, 1941.

MARIN COUNTY CIVIC CENTER, p. 71—Veterans' Memorial Auditorium, completed 1972.

Notes

❖❖❖ The WRIGHT Places in California ❖❖❖

PAGE	CITY	STRUCTURE
9	LOS ANGELES	Aline Barnsdall House ✶ (Hollyhock House)
13	PASADENA	Alice Millard House (La Miniatura)
17	LOS ANGELES	Charles Ennis House ✶
21	HOLLYWOOD	Samuel Freeman House ✶
25	HOLLYWOOD	John Storer House
29	BEVERLY HILLS	Anderton Court Shops ✶
33	BRENTWOOD	George D. Sturges House
37	MALIBU	Arch Oboler Gatehouse/Studio
41	MONTECITO	George C. Stewart House
44	Area Maps	
47	SAN LUIS OBISPO	Kundert Medical Clinic ✶
51	CARMEL	Clinton Walker House
55	PALO ALTO	Paul and Jean Hanna House ✶ (Honeycomb House)
59	ATHERTON	Arthur C. Mathews House
63	SAN FRANCISCO	V. C. Morris Gift Shop ✶
67	SAN ANSELMO	Robert Berger House
71	SAN RAFAEL	Marin County Civic Center ✶
75	BERKELEY	Hilary and Joe Feldman House
79	REDDING	Pilgrim Congregational Church ✶
82	Other Sites	
83	Ancillary Buildings	

✶ Indicates sites open to the public or where regularly scheduled or limited and special tours are offered, as noted in this guide book. The others are private residences that can be viewed from the road.